# HAL•LEONARD
## INSTRUMENTAL PLAY-ALONG

AUDIO
ACCESS
INCLUDED

**PLAYBACK+**
Speed • Pitch • Balance • Loop

# TENOR SAX

# VIDEO GAME MUSIC

Audio arrangements by Peter Deneff

To access audio visit:
**www.halleonard.com/mylibrary**

Enter Code
4765-3371-8535-2867

ISBN 978-1-5400-3603-2

Visit Hal Leonard Online at
**www.halleonard.com**

Contact us:
**Hal Leonard**
7777 West Bluemound Road
Milwaukee, WI 53213
Email: info@halleonard.com

In Europe, contact:
**Hal Leonard Europe Limited**
42 Wigmore Street
Marylebone, London, W1U 2RN
Email: info@halleonardeurope.com

In Australia, contact:
**Hal Leonard Australia Pty. Ltd.**
4 Lentara Court
Cheltenham, Victoria, 3192 Australia
Email: info@halleonard.com.au

# ANGRY BIRDS
## Theme

TENOR SAX

By ARI PULKKINEN

# ASSASSIN'S CREED III
## Main Title

TENOR SAX

By LORNE BALFE

# ASSASSIN'S CREED REVELATIONS
## Theme

TENOR SAX

By LORNE BALFE

# BATTLEFIELD 1942
## Theme

TENOR SAX

By JOEL ERIKSSON

# CIVILIZATION IV
### Baba Yetu

TENOR SAX

Words and Music by
CHRISTOPHER TIN

# DELTARUNE™
## Don't Forget

TENOR SAX

Words and Music by
TOBY FOX

# ELDER SCROLLS IV: OBLIVION
## Main Theme

TENOR SAX

By JEREMY SOULE

# ELDER SCROLLS V: SKYRIM
## Dragonborn Theme

TENOR SAX

By JEREMY SOULE

# FALLOUT®4
## Theme

TENOR SAX

Composed by INON ZUR

# FINAL FANTASY VII
## Main Theme

TENOR SAX

By NOBUO UEMATSU

# FULL METAL ALCHEMIST
### Bratja (Brothers)

TENOR SAX

Words and Music by MICHIRU OSHIMA,
SEIJI MIZUSHIMA and TATIANA NAUMOVA

# IL-2 STURMOVIK: BIRDS OF PREY
## Main Theme

TENOR SAX

By JEREMY SOULE

# SPLINTER CELL: CONVICTION

TENOR SAX

Words and Music by KAVEH COHEN
and MICHAEL NIELSEN

# UNDERTALE®
## Megalovania

TENOR SAX

Music by TOBY FOX

## The Beatles

All You Need Is Love • Blackbird • Day Tripper • Eleanor Rigby • Get Back • Here, There and Everywhere • Hey Jude • I Will • Let It Be • Lucy in the Sky with Diamonds • Ob-La-Di, Ob-La-Da • Penny Lane • Something • Ticket to Ride • Yesterday.

| | | |
|---|---|---|
| _____ 00225330 | Flute | $14.99 |
| _____ 00225331 | Clarinet | $14.99 |
| _____ 00225332 | Alto Sax | $14.99 |
| _____ 00225333 | Tenor Sax | $14.99 |
| _____ 00225334 | Trumpet | $14.99 |
| _____ 00225335 | Horn | $14.99 |
| _____ 00225336 | Trombone | $14.99 |
| _____ 00225337 | Violin | $14.99 |
| _____ 00225338 | Viola | $14.99 |
| _____ 00225339 | Cello | $14.99 |

## Chart Hits

All About That Bass • All of Me • Happy • Radioactive • Roar • Say Something • Shake It Off • A Sky Full of Stars • Someone like You • Stay with Me • Thinking Out Loud • Uptown Funk.

| | | |
|---|---|---|
| _____ 00146207 | Flute | $12.99 |
| _____ 00146208 | Clarinet | $12.99 |
| _____ 00146209 | Alto Sax | $12.99 |
| _____ 00146210 | Tenor Sax | $12.99 |
| _____ 00146211 | Trumpet | $12.99 |
| _____ 00146212 | Horn | $12.99 |
| _____ 00146213 | Trombone | $12.99 |
| _____ 00146214 | Violin | $12.99 |
| _____ 00146215 | Viola | $12.99 |
| _____ 00146216 | Cello | $12.99 |

## Disney Greats

Arabian Nights • Hawaiian Roller Coaster Ride • It's a Small World • Look Through My Eyes • Yo Ho (A Pirate's Life for Me) • and more.

| | | |
|---|---|---|
| _____ 00841934 | Flute | $12.99 |
| _____ 00841935 | Clarinet | $12.99 |
| _____ 00841936 | Alto Sax | $12.99 |
| _____ 00841937 | Tenor Sax | $12.95 |
| _____ 00841938 | Trumpet | $12.99 |
| _____ 00841939 | Horn | $12.99 |
| _____ 00841940 | Trombone | $12.99 |
| _____ 00841941 | Violin | $12.99 |
| _____ 00841942 | Viola | $12.99 |
| _____ 00841943 | Cello | $12.99 |
| _____ 00842078 | Oboe | $12.99 |

## The Greatest Showman

Come Alive • From Now On • The Greatest Show • A Million Dreams • Never Enough • The Other Side • Rewrite the Stars • This Is Me • Tightrope.

| | | |
|---|---|---|
| _____ 00277389 | Flute | $14.99 |
| _____ 00277390 | Clarinet | $14.99 |
| _____ 00277391 | Alto Sax | $14.99 |
| _____ 00277392 | Tenor Sax | $14.99 |
| _____ 00277393 | Trumpet | $14.99 |
| _____ 00277394 | Horn | $14.99 |
| _____ 00277395 | Trombone | $14.99 |
| _____ 00277396 | Violin | $14.99 |
| _____ 00277397 | Viola | $14.99 |
| _____ 00277398 | Cello | $14.99 |

## Movie and TV Music

The Avengers • Doctor Who XI • Downton Abbey • Game of Thrones • Guardians of the Galaxy • Hawaii Five-O • Married Life • Rey's Theme (from *Star Wars: The Force Awakens*) • The X-Files • and more.

| | | |
|---|---|---|
| _____ 00261807 | Flute | $12.99 |
| _____ 00261808 | Clarinet | $12.99 |
| _____ 00261809 | Alto Sax | $12.99 |
| _____ 00261810 | Tenor Sax | $12.99 |
| _____ 00261811 | Trumpet | $12.99 |
| _____ 00261812 | Horn | $12.99 |
| _____ 00261813 | Trombone | $12.99 |
| _____ 00261814 | Violin | $12.99 |
| _____ 00261815 | Viola | $12.99 |
| _____ 00261816 | Cello | $12.99 |

## 12 Pop Hits

Believer • Can't Stop the Feeling • Despacito • It Ain't Me • Look What You Made Me Do • Million Reasons • Perfect • Send My Love (To Your New Lover) • Shape of You • Slow Hands • Too Good at Goodbyes • What About Us.

| | | |
|---|---|---|
| _____ 00261790 | Flute | $12.99 |
| _____ 00261791 | Clarinet | $12.99 |
| _____ 00261792 | Alto Sax | $12.99 |
| _____ 00261793 | Tenor Sax | $12.99 |
| _____ 00261794 | Trumpet | $12.99 |
| _____ 00261795 | Horn | $12.99 |
| _____ 00261796 | Trombone | $12.99 |
| _____ 00261797 | Violin | $12.99 |
| _____ 00261798 | Viola | $12.99 |
| _____ 00261799 | Cello | $12.99 |

## Songs from Frozen, Tangled and Enchanted

Do You Want to Build a Snowman? • For the First Time in Forever • Happy Working Song • I See the Light • In Summer • Let It Go • Mother Knows Best • That's How You Know • True Love's First Kiss • When Will My Life Begin • and more.

| | | |
|---|---|---|
| _____ 00126921 | Flute | $14.99 |
| _____ 00126922 | Clarinet | $14.99 |
| _____ 00126923 | Alto Sax | $14.99 |
| _____ 00126924 | Tenor Sax | $14.99 |
| _____ 00126925 | Trumpet | $14.99 |
| _____ 00126926 | Horn | $14.99 |
| _____ 00126927 | Trombone | $14.99 |
| _____ 00126928 | Violin | $14.99 |
| _____ 00126929 | Viola | $14.99 |
| _____ 00126930 | Cello | $14.99 |

## Top Hits

Adventure of a Lifetime • Budapest • Die a Happy Man • Ex's & Oh's • Fight Song • Hello • Let It Go • Love Yourself • One Call Away • Pillowtalk • Stitches • Writing's on the Wall.

| | | |
|---|---|---|
| _____ 00171073 | Flute | $12.99 |
| _____ 00171074 | Clarinet | $12.99 |
| _____ 00171075 | Alto Sax | $12.99 |
| _____ 00171106 | Tenor Sax | $12.99 |
| _____ 00171107 | Trumpet | $12.99 |
| _____ 00171108 | Horn | $12.99 |
| _____ 00171109 | Trombone | $12.99 |
| _____ 00171110 | Violin | $12.99 |
| _____ 00171111 | Viola | $12.99 |
| _____ 00171112 | Cello | $12.99 |

## Wicked

As Long As You're Mine • Dancing Through Life • Defying Gravity • For Good • I'm Not That Girl • Popular • The Wizard and I • and more.

| | | |
|---|---|---|
| _____ 00842236 | Flute | $12.99 |
| _____ 00842237 | Clarinet | $12.99 |
| _____ 00842238 | Alto Saxophone | $12.99 |
| _____ 00842239 | Tenor Saxophone | $11.95 |
| _____ 00842240 | Trumpet | $12.99 |
| _____ 00842241 | Horn | $12.99 |
| _____ 00842242 | Trombone | $12.99 |
| _____ 00842243 | Violin | $12.99 |
| _____ 00842244 | Viola | $12.99 |
| _____ 00842245 | Cello | $12.99 |

## HAL•LEONARD®

# 101 SONGS

## BIG COLLECTIONS OF FAVORITE SONGS ARRANGED FOR SOLO INSTRUMENTALISTS.

### 101 BROADWAY SONGS

| | | |
|---|---|---|
| 00154199 | Flute | $14.99 |
| 00154200 | Clarinet | $14.99 |
| 00154201 | Alto Sax | $14.99 |
| 00154202 | Tenor Sax | $14.99 |
| 00154203 | Trumpet | $14.99 |
| 00154204 | Horn | $14.99 |
| 00154205 | Trombone | $14.99 |
| 00154206 | Violin | $14.99 |
| 00154207 | Viola | $14.99 |
| 00154208 | Cello | $14.99 |

### 101 HIT SONGS

| | | |
|---|---|---|
| 00194561 | Flute | $16.99 |
| 00197182 | Clarinet | $16.99 |
| 00197183 | Alto Sax | $16.99 |
| 00197184 | Tenor Sax | $16.99 |
| 00197185 | Trumpet | $16.99 |
| 00197186 | Horn | $16.99 |
| 00197187 | Trombone | $16.99 |
| 00197188 | Violin | $16.99 |
| 00197189 | Viola | $16.99 |
| 00197190 | Cello | $16.99 |

### 101 CHRISTMAS SONGS

| | | |
|---|---|---|
| 00278637 | Flute | $14.99 |
| 00278638 | Clarinet | $14.99 |
| 00278639 | Alto Sax | $14.99 |
| 00278640 | Tenor Sax | $14.99 |
| 00278641 | Trumpet | $14.99 |
| 00278642 | Horn | $14.99 |
| 00278643 | Trombone | $14.99 |
| 00278644 | Violin | $14.99 |
| 00278645 | Viola | $14.99 |
| 00278646 | Cello | $14.99 |

### 101 JAZZ SONGS

| | | |
|---|---|---|
| 00146363 | Flute | $14.99 |
| 00146364 | Clarinet | $14.99 |
| 00146366 | Alto Sax | $14.99 |
| 00146367 | Tenor Sax | $14.99 |
| 00146368 | Trumpet | $14.99 |
| 00146369 | Horn | $14.99 |
| 00146370 | Trombone | $14.99 |
| 00146371 | Violin | $14.99 |
| 00146372 | Viola | $14.99 |
| 00146373 | Cello | $14.99 |

### 101 CLASSICAL THEMES

| | | |
|---|---|---|
| 00155315 | Flute | $14.99 |
| 00155317 | Clarinet | $14.99 |
| 00155318 | Alto Sax | $14.99 |
| 00155319 | Tenor Sax | $14.99 |
| 00155320 | Trumpet | $14.99 |
| 00155321 | Horn | $14.99 |
| 00155322 | Trombone | $14.99 |
| 00155323 | Violin | $14.99 |
| 00155324 | Viola | $14.99 |
| 00155325 | Cello | $14.99 |

### 101 MOVIE HITS

| | | |
|---|---|---|
| 00158087 | Flute | $14.99 |
| 00158088 | Clarinet | $14.99 |
| 00158089 | Alto Sax | $14.99 |
| 00158090 | Tenor Sax | $14.99 |
| 00158091 | Trumpet | $14.99 |
| 00158092 | Horn | $14.99 |
| 00158093 | Trombone | $14.99 |
| 00158094 | Violin | $14.99 |
| 00158095 | Viola | $14.99 |
| 00158096 | Cello | $14.99 |

### 101 DISNEY SONGS

| | | |
|---|---|---|
| 00244104 | Flute | $16.99 |
| 00244106 | Clarinet | $16.99 |
| 00244107 | Alto Sax | $16.99 |
| 00244108 | Tenor Sax | $16.99 |
| 00244109 | Trumpet | $16.99 |
| 00244112 | Horn | $16.99 |
| 00244120 | Trombone | $16.99 |
| 00244121 | Violin | $16.99 |
| 00244125 | Viola | $16.99 |
| 00244126 | Cello | $16.99 |

### 101 POPULAR SONGS

| | | |
|---|---|---|
| 00224722 | Flute | $16.99 |
| 00224723 | Clarinet | $16.99 |
| 00224724 | Alto Sax | $16.99 |
| 00224725 | Tenor Sax | $16.99 |
| 00224726 | Trumpet | $16.99 |
| 00224727 | Horn | $16.99 |
| 00224728 | Trombone | $16.99 |
| 00224729 | Violin | $16.99 |
| 00224730 | Viola | $16.99 |
| 00224731 | Cello | $16.99 |

**HAL•LEONARD®**
www.halleonard.com

*Prices, contents and availability subject to change without notice.*